MW00574896

Color Me!™

RELAX • COLOR • CREATE

new seasons®
a division of Publications International, Ltd.

Louis Weber, CEO
Publications International, Ltd.
8140 Lehigh Avenue
Morton Grove, Illinois 60053

ISBN: 978-1-68022-552-5

Manufactured in China.

8 7 6 5 4 3 2 1

Eat
drink
enjoy

EXPLORE THE UNIVERSE

Enjoy the little things.

Let's get lost in Paradise!

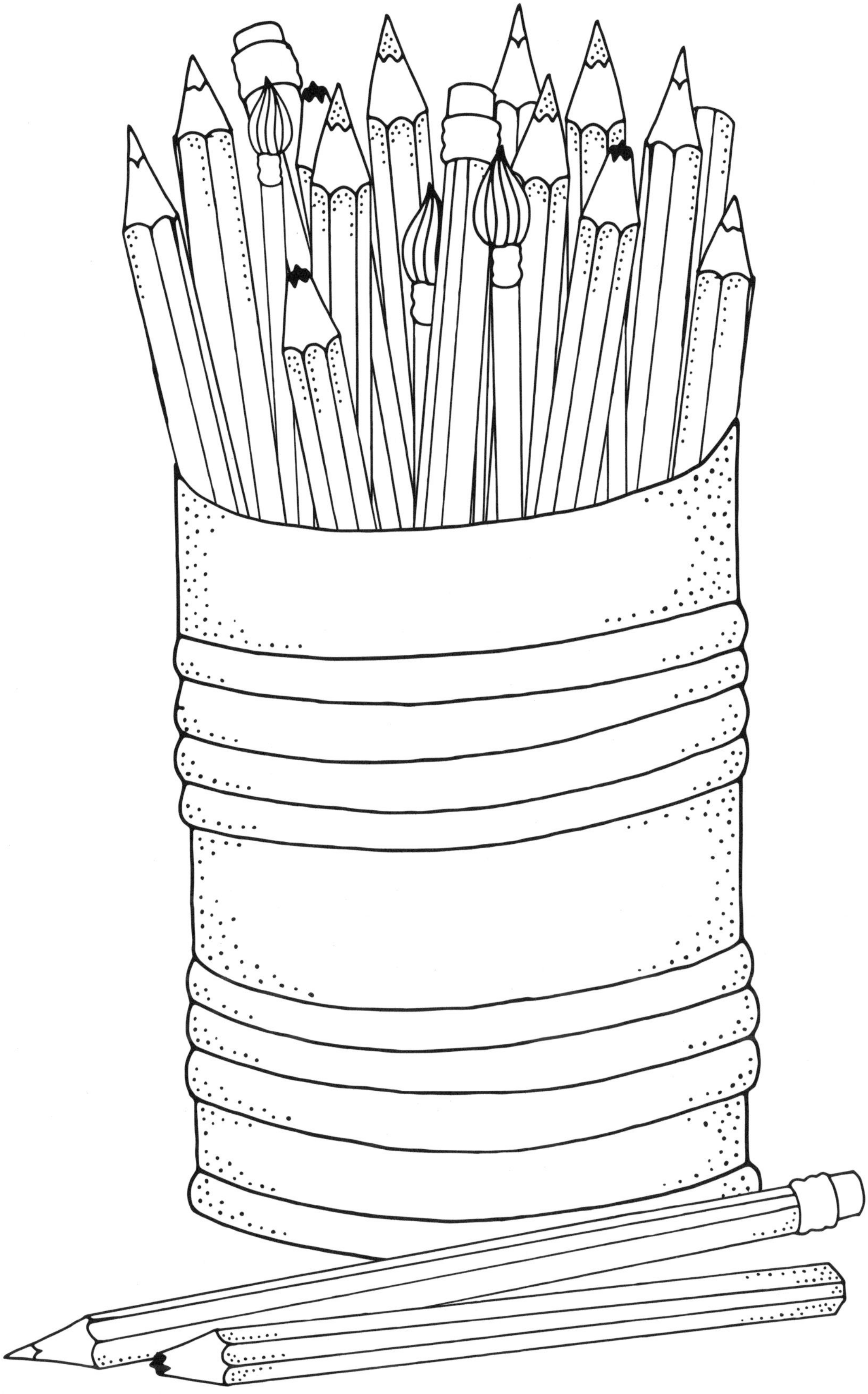

STOP
DREAMING
&
START
DOING

wild & free...